Christmas 1990.   To Mammy
Happy Christmas
From Deirdre
Ian and
Kate

DUBLIN
STOLEN FROM TIME

DUBLIN

STOLEN FROM TIME

Perspectives of Dublin 1790s-1990s

PAT LIDDY

In celebration of
Dublin
European City of Culture 1991

Oisín Art Gallery
In association with
Chadworth Limited
Dublin

James Malton's views are reproduced from copies in the National
Library by kind permission of the Director and Trustees.
Pat Liddy's prints are taken from the originals now held by the
Central Library Department of Dublin Corporation.

First published November 1990
Oisín Art Gallery in association with Chadworth Limited

Text and drawings © Oisín Art Gallery and Pat Liddy
Jacket design by Lou Bowden © Oisín Art Gallery
Layout and design by Donal McNeela, Rory McNeela and Pat Liddy
Co-ordination and distribution by Oisín Art Gallery

Colour Plates: Master Photo Ltd.
Typeset by Printset & Design Ltd.
Printed in Ireland by Microprint Ltd.

Casebound ISBN 0 9512510 31

DEDICATION

*To everyone
who has helped in any way
to preserve restore or enrich
the great City of Dublin.*

Acknowledgements

There were times when I despaired of this book ever seeing the light of day which it certainly would not have without the help of each and all of the following.

My thanks in the first place to my wife Josephine for her advice and unstinted hard work at producing manuscripts to my usual last minute deadlines.

I owe a great deal to my publishers Donal and Rory McNeela for their faith, vision and sheer application to the task of producing this book.

Grateful thanks are due to John Delves, Paul Ennis and David O'Toole of Master Photo Ltd., without whose generous help in the production of the colour separations this book might possibly not have been published.

My thanks also to Peter Delaney and the staff at Microprint who lovingly wet-nursed the book from conception to birth and to Claire Browne who provided a valuable consultancy service.

I cannot forget the support of the Dublin City Centre Business Association, Dublin City Libraries, The National Library and many owners and occupiers of the illustrated buildings.

Lastly, grateful appreciation to Bernard Loughlin for the peace and tranquility of the Tyrone Guthrie Centre, Annaghmakerrig.

Bibliography

The Second City, Patrick Fagan, Branar, Dublin 1986

New Lease of Life, Sean O'Reilly & Nicholas Robinson, The Irish
Architectural Archive, Dublin 1990

Life by the Liffey, John O'Donovan, Gill & Macmillan, Dublin 1986

The Book of the Liffey, Elizabeth Healy, Wolfhound Press, Dublin 1988

James Malton's Dublin Views, Maurice Craig, Dolmen Press, Dublin 1981

Guide to Historic Dublin, Adrian MacLoughlin, Gill and Macmillan,
Dublin 1979

Dublin, Peter Somerville-Large, Granada Publishing Co., London 1979

Dublin 1660-1860, Maurice Craig, Allen Figgis & Co., Dublin 1980

Publisher's Note regarding Prints

Rather than remove the colour pages from this book a limited number of all the colour prints is available and may be ordered by contacting:

Oisín Art Gallery,
44 Westland Row,
Dublin 2.
Tel: 611315
Fax: 610464

Oisín Art Gallery,
10 Marino Mart,
Dublin 3.
Tel: 333456
Fax: 335197

List of Colour Plates

Contents

Introduction

Dublin is exceptional for many reasons not least for its wealth of Georgian architecture. The eighteenth century was a time of elegant expansion which motivated an energetic, some might even say ruthless, policy of sweeping aside the compact medieval city in favour of generous boulevards and gracious mansions.

Not all was magnificence for during these years the level of poverty in the back streets and other deprived areas was growing at an ever increasing pace. To borrow another title, Dublin was indeed a tale of two cities.

Much of the Georgian splendour became tarnished in the next century and by the formation of the Free State in the 1920s many of the once-proud terraces were nothing better than tenements. During the 1960s and 1970s the survival rate of these and indeed of many worthy buildings was low when they fell prey to mindless crass developments which are now subjects of deep regret.

Despite the destruction it is still a wonder that many of the more distinctive eighteenth century buildings are still with us and for the most part have been beautifully restored. James Malton, a London draughtsman, took away his impressions of Dublin to his native city in 1791 and over the next few years produced his famous series of 25 prints for "A Picturesque and Descriptive View of the City of Dublin". Of Malton's total, 24 are still more or less intact, the exception (the Tholsel) was actually demolished in 1806!

Dublin escaped the worst ravages of the Second World War and while there was not always an active awareness to preserve our 18th century legacies the scale of their survival is still fairly unique for any European Capital. More by default than design our Capital's heritage has been **STOLEN FROM TIME.**

It was to record this happy occurance, to honour the more recent efforts of preservation and to help ensure the future that I undertook this present work.

In general I have left it to the individual reader to compare the pictures and ascertain the topographical and social changes which have occurred over a span of two centuries.

I have, where possible, taken the views from Malton's own perspective and have attempted to also include contemporary street life and social comment much in the same way as my esteemed predecessor so eloquently did.

Pat Liddy
Dublin
November 1990

The Life and Times of James Malton

James Malton was the son of Thomas Malton a London-born architectural draughtsman who had settled in Dublin in 1785. Ten years earlier Thomas had published "A Complete Treatise on Perspective" which didn't achieve the targeted sales and forced him to later flee his creditors. In Dublin he scarcely eked out an existance as a teacher of geometry and perspective.

One drawing known to have been executed by him is that of the inside of St. Peter's Cathedral in Waterford. He died in Dublin in 1801 at the age of seventy five.

Thomas Malton had three sons: Thomas the younger, William and James. His son Thomas lived for a time with his father in Dublin but spent most of his life in London where he produced his famous work, "A Picturesque Tour Through the Cities of London and Westminster"; a series illustrated with a hundred aquatint plates.

Born in the 1760s, the exact date is unknown, James Malton followed into his father's profession. As can be judged by his later work he was an accomplished draughtsman. Thomas Malton Senior, in spite of an earlier row with James Gandon, the most prominent architect of the day working in Dublin, succeeded in 1781 in having his son James engaged in Gandon's office. At this time Gandon was heavily involved in the building of the Custom House and Malton, had he performed satisfactorily, would have had secure and valuable employment. However within three years Gandon felt compelled to dismiss James for breaches of conduct and confidence and from that point no further contact was ever made between Gandon and the Maltons. This proved inconvenient for James as will be seen later.

James went on to concentrate on teaching perspective and producing drawings of notable buildings in Dublin. In 1791 he gathered together all his notes, drawings and architectural plans of his chosen subjects and departed for London where over the next eight years he published his now famous twenty five "Picturesque and Descriptive Views of the City of Dublin". They were reproduced in etching and aquatint and publication began in 1792. There were six sets of four views at a guinea a set. The second set contained an extra plate, that of Trinity College Library, Malton's only interior view.

Malton states in his preface that "the entire of the views were taken in 1791 yet as work was in hand till 1797 such alterations as occured in each subject between the taking and publishing of any view of it, have been attended to". Yet if he did revisit Dublin from time to time he failed on account of his soured relationship with Gandon to get any updated plans of the latter's Custom House and Four Courts. As a result his drawings of both of these subjects contain inaccuracies. For instance there are niches on the ground floor wings of the Four Courts where there should be windows and the drum and dome of the building is too small. He also omitted the urns from the corner pavilions of the Custom House (as also did this writer because they had been removed for restoration at the time of drawing).

From 1792 until his death from brain fever in 1803 Malton regularly exhibited in the Royal Academy where his craftsmanship and eye for detail were obviously appreciated. Many of his Dublin scenes were among the works exhibited.

Because Dublin was a city of such social contrasts Malton was highly selective in his chosen subjects. He studiously avoided run-down areas (for example Christ Church Cathedral was not featured because tenement houses were built right against its walls) as there would be little profit in trying to find prospective customers for those prints. Slums and blighted former glories were never far away and Malton could not and probably did not want to altogether exclude some references to them. His street scenes are peopled not only with the grandees in high fashion but also with beggars, servants, shoeless children and mangy dogs.

However on the whole he prefers to show a city of wide (and too clean?) streets, monumental public buildings, elegant mansions, and wide expanses of sky.

Notwithstanding this deliberate discrimination Malton's views are as important a legacy to Dublin as the very buildings he depicted and are an invaluble source of reference of the life and times of eighteenth century Dublin.

A

Picturesque AND Descriptive

View of the City of

DUBLIN

In a Series of the most Interesting Scenes taken in the Year 1791

By James Malton

With

A brief authentic History from the earliest accounts to the

Present Time

Views
of
Present Day Dublin

by

Pat Liddy

DUBLIN
1991
EUROPEAN CITY of CULTURE

1

Dublin Castle (Upper Castle Yard)

On a hill overlooking the little Viking settlement of Dyflin the Vikings built a fort. The same spot was chosen nearly four hundred years later to build the castle ordered by King John of England "for the custody of our treasure and for the administration of Justice".

By 1228 the Castle, with a number of strong towers, walls and a ditch, was complete. The river Poddle obliged by protecting the south and east walls while a massive ditch sixty feet wide and thirty feet deep ran along the remaining sides.

Apart from a couple of sieges, which were successfully repelled, the Castle settled down to administer those parts of Ireland in which the English held sway. Its buildings were used for meetings of Parliament, the Privy Council and the Courts of Law and the Viceroys were expected to live within the walls.

At various times it was felt necessary to repair and strengthen the fortifications, but the dreary black calpstone castle, never a piece of striking beauty and grandeur, was not a popular residence for the Viceroys. In 1684 much of the old castle was pulled down after a fire and plans were soon prepared for a worthy palace by the Surveyor-General, Sir William Robinson. The Record Tower and the Birmingham Tower were about the sum total of what remained above ground of the medieval castle.

From the middle of the 18th century the buildings shown in Malton's scene, including the State Apartments on the left and the Bedford Tower flanked by the two gateways on the right, were built.

Throughout the Georgian period the Castle was the social centre of Dublin. The nobility and rich all flocked to the presence of the Viceroy seeking his patronage or indulging in the great banquets, State occasions, all night balls and gambling (illegal elsewhere in the city).

II

After the Act of Union in 1800 the Castle was consolidated in its role as administrative centre for the Government and was also the headquarters for the policing of the country. The Viceroys and their entourages continued their glittering existences. At times the authorities within became paranoid about rebel mutterings beyond the walls.

Seditious manoeuverings by the native Irish finally burst upon an unwary Dublin Castle when in 1916 a half-hearted attempt was made by insurgents to capture the fortress. The planned take-over failed but the Government's respite lasted only another six years when in 1922 the last Viceroy handed over the Castle to the representatives of the Provisional Irish Government.

The Castle, which had seen so much pageantry in the past was not to be totally denied in the future. It is now the venue for Presidential inaugurations, state banquets and receptions and is used for meetings of the heads of Government of the European Community when Ireland holds the Presidency.

A number of important refurbishments were carried out in the 50s and 60s but in 1985 a massive restoration was begun by the Office of Public Works.

The works consisted of the conservation and restoration of the buildings forming the northern and western blocks of the Upper Courtyard and the construction of a new Conference Hall with appropriate facilities. A new entrance complete with bridge over a moat at Castle Street and a new catering block and press area were also provided. The buildings known as Blocks 8, 9 and 10 situated beside City Hall have been reconstructed as office accommodation. The design approach was to conserve as much as possible and where this was not possible to take down and rebuild.

The statues of Justice and Fortitude over the gateways were also restored. These casts are by the renowned sculptor Jan Van Nost the Younger and the statues have been part of Dublin Castle for more than two hundred years. The upper storey on the Bedford Tower was removed so that it again appears as it was in Malton's print. The only appreciable difference between the two prints is the absence of the spire of St. Werburgh's Church. It was removed in the early 19th century as it was feared that it would provide a vantage point for snipers.

SHIP STREET ENTRANCE TO DUBLIN CASTLE

UPPER CASTLE YARD, DUBLIN CASTLE 1792

UPPER CASTLE YARD, DUBLIN CASTLE 1990

2

BANK OF IRELAND
(THE PARLIAMENT HOUSE)

I

Chichester House in College Green, used by the Irish Parliament since the 16th century, was falling into some ruin so the honourable members resolved to build themselves debating chambers worthy of their exhalted status. In 1727 £6,000 was voted for the new building and a member of Parliament, architect Edward Pearce, was chosen to execute the design. The new legislature would be the first in the world to contain an Upper and Lower House.

Work started a year later and was completed in 1735. Pearce did not live to see his masterpiece which was acclaimed far and wide and engendered not a little envy from the members of the English Parliment in London. A 1780s view of the original Commons is shown in Wheatley's oil painting now in the Leeds City Art Gallery.

By the mid 1780s James Gandon, architect also of the Four Courts and the Custom House, had added a portico extension to the Westmoreland Street side. Disaster struck in 1792, a year before the date of Malton's handiwork, when a fire, started by the heating system, badly damaged the House of Commons. Rebuilding took another four years.

Malton drafted his views with a commercial eye on selling the prints and in this case he had targeted the rich Members of Parliament. However, he made one error of judgement in which he overlooked the sensibilities of his potential buyers. True to the scene as he saw it he included a drover and his dog driving along a column of three pigs. The appalled Parliamentarians gave him the thumbs down and he sensibly removed the pigs but left behind still slightly visible smudge type marks where the picture was reworked.

A colonnade was added to the Foster Place side in 1794 but further improvements were destined to wait until the building no longer functioned as a legislature. Six years later the fateful Act of Union dissolved the Irish Parliament and in 1802 the Bank of Ireland acquired ownership of the premises for £40,000.

The English Government gave strict orders to the bank to remove all evidence of the presence of the former Parliament and Francis Johnson was commissioned to carry out the new designs. Conversion did remove the House of Commons but the bank managed to totally preserve the House of Lords. This chamber, now unique in the world, contains two original tapestries dating from 1733 which represent "The Glorious Battle of the Boyne" and the "Glorious Defence of Londonderry". Also preserved is the mace of the House of Commons bought back for £3,100 in 1937 at a sale in Christie's. The great chandelier, comprising 1,233 pieces of glass, was made in 1788.

Still existing in the tympanum of the central pediment is the Royal Coat of Arms and over the pediment the statues, absent from Malton's print, of Fidelity, Hibernia and Commerce. In a major restoration commenced in 1971 any perished stonework was replaced by stone from the same quarries as the originals and the worn down heads of the statues were newly carved by sculptor Paddy Roe.

College Green remained the headquarters of the Bank of Ireland until its new head office was opened at Lower Baggot Street in 1971. The old Parliament House is still the bank's main Dublin branch.

With arm outstretched a bronze Henry Grattan authoritively presides over College Green as the man himself once held forth in the old Parliament so much so that it became known as Grattan's Parliament.

FOSTER PLACE

PARLIAMENT HOUSE, DUBLIN 1793

BANK OF IRELAND, COLLEGE GREEN, DUBLIN 1990

3

Trinity College

In the late 16th century an attempt was made to establish a Protestant university at St. Patrick's Cathedral. This idea failed, especially due to the opposition of Archbishop Adam Loftus (later Trinity's first Provost), and so another site was sought. This was found on a marshy plot way outside the crumbling city walls beside Hoggen (now College) Green, a common pasturage and sometimes execution ground. Once comprising the great Augustinian Priory of All Hallows, the lands had been granted to the Corporation on the dissolution of the monasteries.

With a charter granted by Queen Elizabeth construction started on the new university in 1592 and the first students were admitted two years later. Nothing remains today of these early red-bricked buildings (drawings of them still exist, though) and the present West Front, featured in Malton's picture, was built between 1752 and 1759 and is attributed to Theodore Jacobson. It is a striking frontage and is especially set off by the two elegant end pavilions. Built of Irish granite and Portland stone and although currently in need of a good cleaning the facade never deserved James Joyce's scathing description of it as "a surly front, a dull stone set in the ring of the city's ignorance".

For the first two hundred years or more the students of Trinity, usually the sons of the nobility and gentry, excelled themselves as revellers, inciters of riots and street fights, political troublemakers, gamblers and instigators of civic misdemeanours rather than as earnest scholars. The student population was tiny at the outset, perhaps no more than 200, with an entrance age as low as thirteen years.

II

Very little change has taken place to the West Front facade of Trinity College in the intervening years since Malton. The building, of course, has aged more and atmospheric pollution has exacted a toll. The low railings around the College were replaced in the last century by the higher and more decorative version familiar today. They were manufactured in the famous ironfoundry of Richard Turner.

The statues now flanking the approach to the entrance are those of two former alumni, Oliver Goldsmith and Edmund Burke. The sculptor was John Henry Foley responsible also for Henry Grattan facing across College Green and the Daniel O'Connell monument in O'Connell Street.

The Georgian houses in Grafton Street and College Green on the right of Malton's depiction are now largely gone and have been replaced by some rather fine Victorian buildings and a few ignoble examples of more modern architecture.

If Trinity College started with less than 200 students the number has now risen to over 6,000 spread over a campus of 42 acres. Its past luminaries included the statesmen Henry Grattan and Edmund Burke, patriots Wolfe Tone and Thomas Davis, first President of Ireland Douglas Hyde, literary geniuses Jonathan Swift, Samuel Beckett, Oliver Goldsmith and Oscar Wilde, philosopher George Berkeley, historian William Lecky, mathematician William Rowan Hamilton, medical pioneers William Stokes and Denis Burkitt and physicists George Francis Fitzgerald and Nobel prizewinner Ernest Walton.

TRINITY CAMPANILE

15

TRINITY COLLEGE, DUBLIN 1793

TRINITY COLLEGE, DUBLIN 1990

4

Trinity Library

I

There was a library from the earliest days at Trinity. The first one, built over the students' chambers, had a gallery with pews supplied for the readers.

It became apparent over the next century that a much more commodius accommodation was needed so by 1712 the foundation stone was laid for the grand new library building. Designed by Thomas Burgh the building contained a reading room which at two hundred and ten feet long and forty one feet broad was the largest in Europe. Oak partitions divided the room into shelved compartments.

Over the compartments ran an extensive gallery with busts by Scheemakers, Simon Vierpyl and Roubilliac surmounting the balustrade. The ceiling was flat then and stood at forty feet above floor level.

The land on which Trinity College was built was extremely marshy so to keep the new library damp-free it was erected over an open arcaded ground floor.

II

A major alteration to the Library came in the 1860s when architects Thomas Deane and Benjamin Woodword almost doubled its size by constructing upper level compartments and converting the ceiling from a flat surface into high barrel-vaulting. The modifications created a library of immense size. In the 1890s the arcaded ground floor was glazed and additional library space was thus created.

Despite the capacity (200,000 volumes) of what is now known as the Old Library the increase in students and faculties called for the construction of more space elsewhere on the college grounds. New libraries include the Berkeley (designed by Koralek, 1967), the Lecky (designed by Ahrends, Burton and Koralek, 1978) and the Science (designed by Scott Tallon Walker, 1981).

Trinity College libraries now have the largest collection of books in Ireland, over two and a half million. For nearly 200 years the College has had the right to receive a free copy of every book and publication issued in Great Britain and Ireland.

The Old Library contains the College's most prized possessions including Greek and Latin manuscripts, Egyptian Papyri, 16th and 17th century Irish works and the incomparable medieval Book of Armagh, Book of Durrow and the world famous 9th century Book of Kells.

Trinity's modern Conservation Laboratory is attached to the Old Library.

Although open to the public all year round by far the best time to visit the Old Library is in the off-tourist season when a visitor can take the time to browse (but not touch any books) and soak in the atmosphere of one of Ireland's finest architectural spaces.

OLD LIBRARY, TRINITY COLLEGE

COLLEGE LIBRARY, TRINITY COLLEGE, DUBLIN 1793

OLD LIBRARY, TRINITY COLLEGE, DUBLIN 1990

5

Provost's House

I

The Provost's House in Trinity College may not be the largest of the 18th century's great mansions but it was certainly set out to be one of the most splendid. The interiors were sumptuously designed and decorated and the rooms, especially the salon, were exceptionally spacious and well appointed. The outstanding plasterwork throughout was by Patrick and John Wall.

When Provost Francis Andrews had successfully finalised the building of the main West Front of Trinity College he turned his attention towards his own quarters. Lord Burlington's design for General Wade's house in London was his inspiration for the facade and Andrews employed John Smyth, architect of St. Catherine's Church, to supervise the construction.

Work started in 1769 and was completed at a cost of £11,000. The stone used was imported sandstone and not Portland stone as was more commonly in vogue.

The domed tower to the left of the Provost's House in Malton's picture was part of the chapel. It was even then unstable and was shortly afterwards taken down. The water-barrel cart is probably coming from St. Patrick's Well in Nassau Street which was reputed to provide an excellent water for tea!

Very little alteration was made to the house since it was first constructed. Maintenance has always been kept up and as a result no major restoration was ever necessary. Unlike all of the other great houses in Dublin the Provost's House still remains as a private residence. It is a statutory requirement for the Provost to live there where his administration offices are also located.

Tours of the house are sometimes organised and its facilities are occasionally used with the approval of the Provost who for the last number of years has been Dr. W. A. Watts.

Except for a railings now surmounting the wall the perimeter around the house is unchanged from Malton's day. The gate piers are still original but in 1990 they underwent a major conservation. As with the fabric of the Custom House it was found that the iron clamps holding the outer skin of granite to the brick core were rusting and displacing the stonework.

The bronze statue in the foreground of the modern painting is that of Molly Malone by sculptor Jeanne Rynhart and commissioned by the Jurys Hotel Group for the 1988 Dublin Millennium.

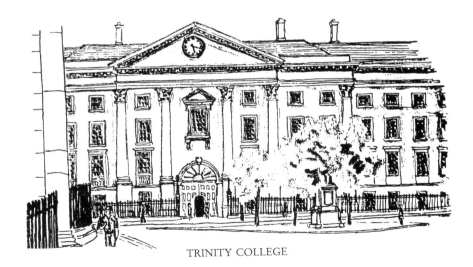

TRINITY COLLEGE

PROVOST'S HOUSE, TRINITY COLLEGE, DUBLIN 1794

PROVOST'S HOUSE, TRINITY COLLEGE, DUBLIN 1990

6

St. Patrick's Cathedral

I

St. Patrick, according to ancient manuscripts, baptised converts at the site of a well nearby where a small wooden church dedicated to him was later erected. This holy well was venerated until the period just after the Reformation.

After the Anglo-Norman invasion the newly imposed Archbishop of Dublin, John Comyn, a Benedictine monk, had plans to enlarge and enrich his See. He had no wish to have his ambitions thwarted by living in the palace next to the existing cathedral of Christ Church. Here he might be under the thumbs of the City Provosts and the Augustinian Priory attached to Christ Church.

John Comyn selected a site in the Liberties, an area outside the city jurisdiction and there he built a collegiate church which opened in 1191. The new stone ediface, in fact, replaced the old wooden church of the same name. Henry de Londres, Comyn's successor, raised the status of St. Patrick's to that of a cathedral in 1213. Twelve years later the church was rebuilt as it looks today, the work being completed in 1254. Fire destroyed the original tower, the present one dates from 1370. In 1560, the first public clock in Dublin was erected on this tower.

The Reformation brought a diminution of status to the cathedral when it was reduced to the rank of parish church for a period. It was restored to its former rights in 1555 and on the accession of Queen Elizabeth the liturgy of the English Church was adopted. During the Commonwealth period in England St. Patrick's suffered again. Under Oliver Cromwell courts martial were held here and tradition says that soldiers' horses were stabled in parts of the building.

In 1660 the Cathedral was again rehabilitated and it led a peaceful existence thereafter. But church finances were never sufficient from this period on and by the time Malton drew his elevation the building was structurally in a fairly sorry state.

In some ways the two views of St. Patrick's, separated by two centuries, hardly differ from each other. Malton's painting, however, makes it fairly obvious that the cathedral was badly in need of a thorough restoration. This was in fact carried out by Benjamin Guinness between 1860 and 1864. The result of this work is what we see today.

The wide open space to the side of the cathedral in Malton's view is gone now that St. Patrick's Close divides the former lands attached to the property. On the other hand the houses that encroached upon the Cathedral including those seen to the left and right of the old print were demolished and the beautiful St. Patrick's Park was laid out.

While for the most part Malton was only concerned with exteriors it is the inside of the Cathedral that is the most striking. Around three hundred feet in length and fifty six feet to the nave roof, St. Patrick's is one of the largest churches in Ireland. The various monuments, tablet carvings, vaults and banners encapsulate the very history of Dublin.

St. Patrick's is now one of the principal tourist attractions of Dublin, not least for its connection with Dean Swift (see under No. 7 West Front of St. Patrick's). In 1991, the eight hundredth anniversary of the Cathdral, there are plans formulated by the present Dean, Victor Griffin, to increase the pedestrian precincts around the West Front and along St. Patrick's Close. This will have the effect of unifying the whole Cathedral complex comprising the Cathedral itself, the Deanery, the schools and the Library (Marsh's Library — the oldest public library in Ireland) thus preserving a tradition of the ancient monasteries of Ireland.

ENTRANCE TO MARSH'S LIBRARY

SAINT PATRICK'S CATHEDRAL, DUBLIN 1793

SAINT PATRICK'S CATHEDRAL, DUBLIN 1990

7

West Front of St. Patrick's Cathedral

I

St. Patrick's was always outside the commercial and civic centre of Dublin. In the late 18th century there was almost nothing of note in the vicinity of the cathedral except the slums of the socially deprived and the impoverished working classes. It had been a relatively prosperous district a century earlier when local businesses including a substantial weaving industry thrived but this had changed disasterously when a number of penal trade restrictions in 1699 plunged thousands of families into destitution. The slums of the Liberties became lengendary.

Johnathan Swift, Dean of St. Patrick's from 1713 until his death in 1745, when not writing his tracts and famous classics such as Gulliver's Travels, busied himself in attending to the pressing needs of his parishioners. Dean Swift was born in Hoey's Court beside Werburgh Street and when he died after a long illness he was buried at midnight in the south west of the nave of the Cathedral beside his beloved Stella.

Swift had done his best to keep repairs and maintenance on the agenda but by Malton's time serious defects were becoming more pronounced on the Cathedral's fabric. Possible philantrophic rescue of the building never manifested itself in the 18th century. Perhaps the undesirable appearance of the whole neighbourhood discouraged sufficient interest in its rehabilitation.

Malton's print is very indicative of the down-at-heel appearance of St. Patrick's and its surroundings. The "Dutch Billy" gabled houses built by the once affluent Huguenots were now housing people in much reduced circumstances. A cattle drover is driving a pair of animals most probably to one of the myriad of small unsanitary abattoirs. There is no pavement and the road has no permanent surface.

II

The downhill spiral in the fortunes of St. Patrick's and its adjacent area continued into the mid 19th century. The population was growing at an alarming rate and several families shared single houses with no sanitation. The narrow fetid alleyways around the cathedral were playgrounds for children, haunts for beggars and a stomping ground for the wretched army of street traders. Disease and the famines of the 1840s left a ghastly toll.

In the 1850s Dean Pakenham did manage a detailed restoration of the Lady Chapel but the main structure was delayed and in great danger. Then just in time between 1860 and 1864 Sir Benjamin Guinness, of the illustrious brewery family, spent the equivalent of several millions of pounds at todays values in completely restoring the Cathedral. His sons Lord Iveagh and Lord Ardilaun continued the work. Were it not for this intervention St. Patrick's would most likely not be standing today.

The Guinness's also cleared away many of the surrounding slums, built magnificent public apartments, placed a park to the north of the Cathedral and provided a roofed market for the street traders.

More restorations have been carried out this century notably in 1972. Plans have now been formulated in which it is proposed to move Patrick Street, which itself is being widened, a further twenty five feet or so away from the West Front. There had been concerns that increased traffic on the new dual carriageway would damage the Cathedral's foundations and this concession will not only protect the church but will give a welcome new plaza area.

It will be noticed from the modern print that the Cathedral, which is built on marshy ground, is by now several feet below the surface of Patrick Street. It is not that the Cathedral is sinking but rather that the road surface has gained more height over the centuries.

In common with general practice in other cathedrals the great West Door is only opened on ceremonial occasions four or five times yearly. Usual entrance is through the south-west doorway from St. Patrick's Close.

BULL ALLEY FROM ST. PATRICK'S PARK

WEST FRONT OF SAINT PATRICK'S CATHEDRAL, DUBLIN 1793

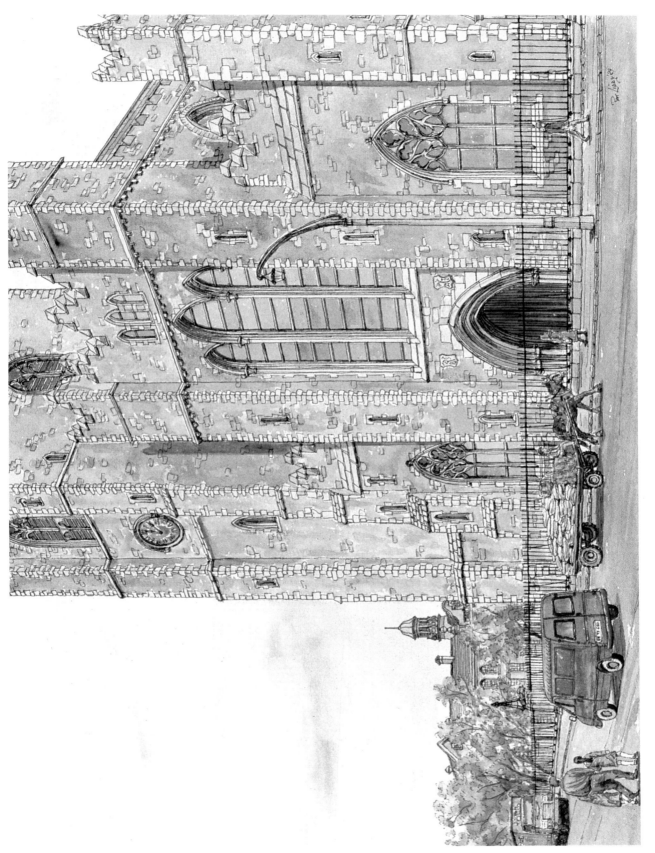

WEST FRONT OF SAINT PATRICK'S CATHEDRAL 1990

8

City Hall (Royal Exchange)

I

Central Dublin in the mid 18th century struggled to emerge from its medieval legacy of narrow streets and cramped lanes. The establishment in 1757 of the Wide Streets Commissioners provided the necessary vehicle to accomplish this objective. Their first task was to lay out Parliament Street as the principal approach from Capel Street Bridge to Dublin Castle. To close off the vista at the head of the new street it was resolved to build an Exchange or Merchants Business Centre and a design competition was held.

Thomas Cooley, a Londoner (as was James Gandon who was placed second), was the winner and his building, erected between 1769 and 1779, is among the very best examples of neo-classicism in the city.

The interior was basically one large open space under an impressive dome supported by a circle of columns. Plasterwork throughout was by a leading Dublin stuccodore Charles Thorp. Total cost was £58,000 and this level of expenditure and the splendid end result reflected the wealth, power and prestige of the Dublin merchants of the time.

Business was conducted and contacts made under the great dome and then the deals were wrapped up in the luxury of the upstairs Coffee Room where the merchants imbibed their expensive beverage which at that time was considered a fashionable if not a snobbish drink.

II

The merchants were unceremoniously ushered out during the Rebellion of 1798 when the Royal Exchange was turned over to the military as an interrogation centre where the cries of the tortured could be heard in the street outside. When matters quietened down the merchants moved back in again but with the adversely changed economic conditions brought about by the Act of Union in 1800 business slackened and by the 1840s there was little justification for continuing the Exchange.

Dublin Corporation were looking for a new home and in 1851 that body purchased the building which a year later became City Hall. The old Coffee Room was converted into the Council Chamber and offices were built around the outer perimeter of the ground floor spoiling somewhat the original open space effect. But the City Hall still remains a gem of Georgian Architecture.

Inside the rotunda can be seen an 18th century mahogony bench from the old Irish House of Commons, Charles Thorp's fine plaster ceiling and the marble floor relaid in 1898 incorporating a circular mosaic depicting the Dublin City Coat-of-Arms. Frescoes around the dome showing scenes from Dublin's history were painted by James Ward between 1914 and 1919. There are also four statues, one by Edward Smyth (that of Dr. Charles Lucas) and the remaining three (Daniel O'Connell, Thomas Drummond and Thomas Davis) by John Hogan.

In its long and chequered history the City Hall also saw many nationalistic gatherings and patriotic funerals, the last of which was that of Michael Collins in August 1922. The front ballustrade once collapsed under the surge of a crowd and several spectators were killed. The present front balcony and railings are a later vintage than those shown in Malton's drawing. The City Hall was occupied for a short time during the uprising of 1916 and it was fortunate that it was not destroyed.

The Lord Mayor's coach parked beside City Hall in the modern view was built by William Whitton of Dublin and made its first appearance in 1791. It is still used for ceremonial occasions.

THE LORD MAYOR'S COACH

ROYAL EXCHANGE, DUBLIN 1792

CITY HALL, DUBLIN 1990

9

The Custom House

I

Before the foundation stone of the present Custom House was laid in 1781 there had been four predecessors. The first was built in 1620, followed shortly in 1637 by another, the third arrived in the 1660s and the Wellington Quay version (shown in Malton's "View from Capel Street") was erected in 1707.

Moving further downriver with each succeeding Custom House, Wellington Quay was still found to be unsuitable for deep draught vessels and the quayside itself could accommodate only one ship at a time. More frustration was caused by the low harbour wall which was sometimes breached by floods thus ruining merchandise stored along the quays.

John Beresford, the Revenue Commissioner, was determined to build a new Custom House nearer to the mouth of the Liffey and persuaded one of England's most promising architects to pass over an invitation to Russia and come to Dublin instead. James Gandon was to leave Dublin a number of important architectural legacies not the least of which is his Custom House which was completed by 1792 at a cost of nearly a quarter of a million pounds.

Laid on a bed of wool and wickerwork to counteract the marshy ground the building of the Custom House was not without incident. Mobs, in the pay of merchants with vested interests who opposed relocation of the Old Custom House, harried the construction workers. For personal protection Gandon himself constantly wore a sword. To add to these difficulties in 1789 a fire broke out and destroyed some of the completed work.

The large Custom House Docks, a series of sheltered berths, were also built at this time but these, located on the eastern side of the Custom House, are out of view in Malton's print.

II

Another fire in 1833 nearly destroyed the Custom House but fortunately it was reconstructed although Gandon's original interior was largely altered. By the mid 1800s this end of the Liffey was bustling with activity and the facilities on offer were at full stretch.

In 1879 a swing bridge was built where the present Butt Bridge stands and a year later the new Carlisle (O'Connell) Bridge was opened. This section of river between the two bridges comprising Eden and Burgh Quays soon fell silent to shipping. As the years further rolled on the increasing size of ships compelled the authorities to build a new deep water harbour at Alexandra Basin and by the turn of the century the Custom House and its adjoining docks were becoming less relevant to Dublin Port.

In 1921 during the War of Independence, the Custom House fell prey to fire once more only this time on a more disastrous scale. The conflageration was so intense that the stone rubble was still cooling six months later. Reconstruction appeared hopeless and the building that had inspired Lutyen's Viceroy's Palace in New Delhi seemed doomed. The basic walls were still standing so it was decided to go ahead. The dome and drum had to be totally rebuilt.

Ireland's best known architectural glory was saved but in the late 70s and 80s it became apparent that resulting from the last fire there was serious deterioration to the fabric of the Custom House. Major repair and conservation works have been going on since 1984 and are due for completion in 1991 at a cost of nearly £6 million.

A substantial quantity of carved stone is now being repaired and replaced. Each of the four Coat of Arms weighs about twelve tons and all were in need of restoration as also were the four roof urns whose function is to mask the chimney flues.

The four statues of Portland stone; Plenty, Neptune, Industry and Mercury, were removed from the south-facing pediment of the Custom House in 1940. The two male figures were carved by Augustine Carlini, a sculptor from Genoa, and the female figures were worked by Edward Smyth who also executed the Riverine Heads which are synonymous with the Custom House. The statues have been carefully restored and replaced this time on the north side of the building.

The restoration works were awarded a Europa Nostra Diploma of Merit in 1989.

ARMS OF IRELAND, CUSTOM HOUSE

THE CUSTOM HOUSE, 1792

THE CUSTOM HOUSE, DUBLIN, 1990

10

The Four Courts (The Law Courts)

I

Property owners and business people with vested interests in the area around the old Custom House vociferously and sometimes violently opposed its replacement by a new and grander version further downriver. Their anger was somewhat assuaged by the promise to situate on Inns Quay an equally imposing ediface. This was to accommodate the Four Courts which badly needed to relocate from entirely unsuitable premises near Christ Church Cathedral. Design would be in the hands of James Gandon, the same architect in charge of the new Custom House.

Thomas Cooley, architect of the Royal Exchange (now the City Hall), had already built a public office on Inns Quay which Gandon now incorporated with some modifications as the West Wing, built a similiar East Wing and joined the two to a central domed core with arches and arcades. The foundation stone was laid by the Viceroy, the Duke of Rutland, in 1786. The first court sessions took place ten years later and by 1802 the whole splendid array was completed.

Financing the project was nearly scuttled by high inflation, rebellion at home and the drain caused by wars in Europe. The final cost stood at around £200,000 (at least £10 million at todays prices not taking into account that wages and other costs were relatively much lower two hundred years ago).

The portico contains six Corinthian columns and over the pediment stand five statues; Moses, Justice, Mercy, Authority and Wisdom. Five courts, not four, sat in Gandon's masterpiece and these were: the Kings Bench, the Chancery, the Exchequer, the Common Pleas and the Judicature.

Untypically Malton's drawing is incorrect in a number of aspects most noticeably in his rendering of the dome which appears smaller and less imposing than it was in reality. With a drum diameter of seventy-six feet it was two and a half times larger than its Custom House counterpart. Malton's discrepancies are mostly due to the incomplete state of the Four Courts before he departed for London and his earlier falling out with Gandon denied him access to up-to-date drawings.

II

Malton took his perspective from Ormonde Bridge which was subsequently swept away in a flood in 1802, the year the Four Courts was completed. The replacement, Richmond (now O'Donovan Rossa) Bridge, was built nearer to Gandon's building and is the bridge in the foreground of the modern print.

The ramshackle but somewhat picturesque houses reaching down to the waterfront, opposite the Four Courts in Malton's picture, were removed shortly afterwards to make way for the rebuilding of Merchant and Wood Quays.

Both of Gandon's riverside glories were destroyed in anger during the violent days of the 1920s. In 1922 the Four Courts was occupied by anti-Treaty forces and was bombarded by Government troops using borrowed British army field guns. A mine then shattered the dome and central block and also destroyed the irreplaceable collection of 800 years of accumulated historical documents held in the adjoining Public Record Office. In the interior, eight statues and other notable carvings by sculptor Edward Smyth were also lost.

Within nine years of the disaster a complete restoration by the Office of Public Works was expertly concluded. The exterior was unchanged from the original except for alterations to the dome which had to be replaced in its entirety. More recent improvements to the complex include the building of an office annexe on the site of the old Four Courts Hotel. The resultant release of office space within the Four Courts itself has allowed refurbishment to be carried out and the provision of additional courtrooms and ancilliary accommodation.

The only boat traffic on this stretch of the Liffey nowadays is the occasional craft from one of the upstream boatclubs. There are plans to run an eighty seat river bus to link Heuston Station with points in the central city.

Additional landmarks erected after Malton's day, including Arran Quay church and the Wellington Monument, are discernable in the current print.

THE FOUR COURTS ARCADE

THE LAW COURTS, DUBLIN 1799

THE FOUR COURTS, DUBLIN 1990

11

Christ Church Place (The Tholsel)

I

The first Tholsel, a meeting place for the city council and other bodies such as merchants who used the building as an exchange, was erected on this spot at Skinner's Row in the early 14th century. It was rebuilt in 1683 in the form seen in Malton's print.

A clock tower and cupola shown in a drawing by Thomas Dineley in 1680 had vanished by Malton's day and indeed the various assemblies had more or less deserted what was by now a building in an advanced state of decay.

The City Recorder's Court held its sessions in the Tholsel where punishments was meeted out by whipping alleged criminals from Skinners' Row to College Green. There was also a whipping post and a pillory in front of the Tholsel but these cruel implements were removed before the 1790s.

Skinner's Row itself had a reputation as a narrow, dirty and busy street where the many small businesses included a large number of booksellers and printers.

One of the duties of the porter in the Tholsel was to act as a fire warden. When a conflagration was reported to him he alerted the Lord Mayor and the Sheriffs and rang the fire bell. A motley crew of firefighters could then be turned out equipped with the Tholsel's two water engines, eight dozen buckets and a supply of large hooks, ladders, pickaxes and shovels.

II

Whatever the criticisms about modern property owners their 18th century counterparts were very neglectful of their duties to adequately maintain their own buildings. The Tholsel, as has already been alluded to, was no exception to this neglect and by 1806 it had to be completely demolished.

Nothing significant was put up in its place and eventually Skinner's Row was widened into Christ Church Place and the Tholsel corner was lost altogether to the also widened Nicholas Street. The building opposite the Tholsel was part of the old Law Courts which moved to the Four Courts in 1796. This structure and its neighbours abutted onto the walls of Christ Church and were pulled down in the 1870s slum clearance and rehabilitation of the Cathedral. The boundary railings of Christ Church are shown in the modern view as is the new office block built by Hillview Securities (behind which is the Tailor's Hall).

The immediate area around the Tholsel itself has been an eyesore for many years but was relieved somewhat in 1988 by the construction of the Peace Park. The latest development agreed for this site is an hotel belonging to the Jurys Group. The author's elevation is based on the architect's (Burke, Kennedy, Doyle) plans for this hotel but planning complications and delays arising from the presence of archaeological remains may regretably lead to the abandonment of the project.

The two statues in the niches over the entrance to the Tholsel and the city stocks were removed to the crypt of Christ Church Cathedral and can still be seen today.

CRYPT, CHRIST CHURCH CATHEDRAL

THE THOLSEL, DUBLIN 1793

CHRISTCHURCH PLACE, DUBLIN 1990

12

The Royal Hospital, Kilmainham

I

With the exception of St. Patrick's Cathedral (largely rebuilt in the 1860s) and the Tholsel (demolished 1806) the Royal Hospital is the oldest of the buildings featured in Malton's collection. It is also one of the finest structures in the country and the only example of 17th century monumental architecture remaining in Dublin.

On land once occupied by a priory of the Knights Templars and later the Knights Hospitallers, it seemed appropriate when in 1680 it was decided to build a hospital and retirement home for infirm and retired soldiers. The idea was the brainchild of the Duke of Ormonde under a charter granted by King Charles II. The institution was inspired by Ormonde's visit to Les Invalides in Paris and as such, preceeding Chelsea by a number of years, Kilmainham and its Parisian counterpart became the world's first military hospitals.

At a cost of £24,000 work was completed in 1684. Initially the hospital was set in lands uninterrupted from those of the Phoenix Park save by the meandering River Liffey. It was an airy location, well isolated from the city where overcrowding, fevers and disease were a constant menace.

Sir William Robinson, at that time Surveyor General in Ireland, designed the Royal Hospital. Architects Thomas Burgh, Sir Edward Lovett Pearce and Francis Johnston were involved in further developments and maintenance.

Malton's print shows the Master's Quarters on the extreme right, the Great Hall in the centre under the Tower, the chapel at the end of the block and the House of the Deputy Adjutant General on the left.

II

The last of the old soldiers to leave the Royal Hospital departed in 1927 when the building itself began to show signs of neglect. Part of the establishment was then used for about two decades as the administrative headquarters of the Garda Síochána until it was finally abandoned except for use as a kind of museum warehouse.

Then in the 1970s it was at last decided to save this historical and architectural gem which by now was falling into a dangerous state of decay. From 1980 to 1984 at a cost of £20 million a massive and thorough restoration was undertaken by the Office of Public Works.

Fortunately Robinson's plans and all subsequent records were still available in the Public Record Office and using these the building was authentically restored. Oak carvings, ceiling plasterwork, stonework, stained glass windows, wood panelling, oak beams and floors all received meticulous attention. The formal gardens, outhouses and driveways were also rehabilitated.

Now open to the public, the Royal Hospital is used for state functions, exhibitions and selected entertainments. It is also being developed as a major centre for culture and the arts. The National Museum has been allocated most of the dormitory wings for display purposes and the building will house the Museum of Modern Art.

In 1986 the scale and success of the preservation works were acknowledged when the Royal Hospital was awarded a gold medal by Europa Nostra.

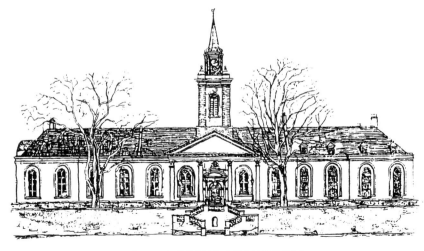

ROYAL HOSPITAL, KILMAINHAM

THE ROYAL HOSPITAL, KILMAINHAM, DUBLIN 1794

THE ROYAL HOSPITAL, KILMAINHAM, DUBLIN 1990

13

Army Headquarters
(Royal Military Infirmary)

I

With the Royal Hospital in Kilmainham unable to meet the increasing needs for the provision of health care for serving soldiers it was decided to build two new military hospitals. One would be sited at Arbour Hill (later to be rebuilt as Saint Bricin's) and the other was to occupy a plot at the eastern end of the Phoenix Park known as Ellen Hore's meadow which before the Reformation held a Dominican Priory.

The Viceroy, the Duke of Rutland, laid the foundation stone in 1786. The infirmary was completed in 1788 at a cost of £9,000 and received its first patients two years later. Design was by Gandon (except for the cupola) who was literally run off his feet with the number of important commissions he was concurrently attending to. Consequently, it could be said that the architecture is unspectacular but it is nevertheless very pleasing. Gandon's plans were executed by William Gibson, architect to the Board of Works.

II

During the 19th century additional buildings were added and in 1851 a new fever hospital was erected. By the turn of the century the facilities in the infirmary were hopelessly outdated and all the patients were transferred in 1913 to a new modern hospital, the King George V Hospital. The former infirmary then became military headquarters for the British Army in Ireland. While the function of the building obviously changed no major restoration or alteration work took place at this time.

Military operations were directed from here during the 1916 Rebellion and Padraig Pearse was also brought here from Moore Street to dictate his order of surrender.

Following the Treaty the British Army were replaced by headquarters staff of the new Irish Army who moved in from Portobello Barracks in 1923. Plans were then formulated for military headquarters, the proposed military college and the civilian Department of Defence to occupy the Royal Hospital in Kilmainham but this move never came to fruition. By 1925 it was decided to leave army headquarters in shared accommodation with the Department of Defence in the old Infirmary.

At the time of writing the building has been temporarily vacated to allow a £2.5 million refurbishment to the Portland stone exterior, the roof and to complete a modern upgrading of the electrics and heating. Sensitive restoration of the interior is also on the agenda.

ARMY HEADQUARTERS

ROYAL MILITARY INFIRMARY, DUBLIN 1794

ARMY HEADQUARTERS, DUBLIN 1990

14

Blackhall Place (Bluecoat Hospital)

I

Through the influence of the Duke of Ormonde a charter was granted in 1670 to found a charitable school for boys coming out of poor families. Called officially the Hospital and Free School of King Charles the Second, Dublin, the school was more commonly referred to as the King's Hospital or the Blue Coat Hospital because of the boys' military style blue uniform.

Land on Oxmanstown Green was donated in 1671 and a building was erected but despite extensive repairs in the 1740s it was deemed only thirty years later to be in acute danger of falling down. Two competitions for a new design were held and although the native profession had for long been overshadowed by English architects it was a Cork man, Thomas Ivory, Master of the School of Architectural Drawing in the Dublin Society, who won through on both occasions.

The governors of the school, under the chairman, Sir Thomas Blackhall, had ambitious plans and Ivory was more than capable of realising them. His drawings, now in the British Library in London, show a monumental arcaded quadrangle behind the front block, the latter surmounted with a tall and gracious steeple as shown in Malton's print. The government refused to spend public money on the scheme and charitable revenues fell far short of target thanks to the more successful fund raising at the rival Rotunda Lying-in Hospital. Plans were modified, the steeple was abandoned at the halfway stage and the quadrangle never saw the light of day. A disgusted Ivory resigned.

On a site adjacent to the old institution the now much curtailed school was opened in December 1783 ten years after the work started. Commencing in 1780 tickets for the Irish State Lottery were drawn by two of the boys from the school.

Nothing much changed over the next century until in 1894 the uncompleted tower was removed and replaced by the present cupola designed by Robert J. Sterling. The Kings Hospital School moved out to Palmerstown in 1968 and the building was placed on the open market. Little interest was shown in it until the Incorporated Law Society, prodded by its President Peter Prentice, of Matheson, Ormsby and Prentice, saw in its acquisition the ideal headquarters for the Society which was then operating from cramped offices in the Four Courts and other scattered locations.

Many hurdles and setbacks had to be overcome before the society finally took possession and began a creditable and painstaking restoration. While the fabric of the building had been reasonably well looked after down the years, a legacy of problems were left by short cuts and substandard work in the latter part of the construction period arising from the diminishing coffers of the school. However, on the 14th of June 1978 Blackhall Place, as its now known, was officially reopened, a triumph of restoration by caring owners.

By a coincidence the Incorporated Law Society, the governing body of solicitors in Ireland, has a pedigree going back to 1773 the same year as the foundation stone of their future headquarters was laid. In that year a statute was enacted to regulate the moral and educational qualifications of apprentices seeking admission as attorneys. This in turn led to the formation of the Society of Attorneys in 1774, the Law Club in 1791 and finally the Law Society of Ireland in 1830 which was incorporated by Royal Charter in 1852.

BLUE COAT SCHOOL, BLACKHALL PLACE

BLUE-COAT HOSPITAL, DUBLIN 1798

INCORPORATED LAW SOCIETY, DUBLIN 1990

15

Rotunda Hospital (Lying-in Hospital)

I

Mother and infant mortality was horrifically high especially among the poor in the early 1700s. Dr. Bartholomew Mosse, a military surgeon turned midwife, who was deeply moved by the often repeated scene of women giving birth by the roadside, opened his first hospital for poor lying-in women in 1745 in a former theatre in George's Lane.

A rather forceful character, Mosse succeeded in leasing four acres of ground called the "Barley Fields" from developer Luke Gardiner and in persuading the top architect of the day, German born Richard Cassels (or Castle), to design his new hospital. Funding would partly come from income generated by the resourceful Mosse who turned the grounds into an extremely fashionable entertainment complex. His assembly rooms and pleasure gardens, with an entrance fee of a shilling, attracted the rich and powerful in great numbers.

Understanding the need to save money Cassels suggested that to reduce his fee he would reuse his previous plans for Leinster House and make whatever modifications which were found to be necessary. This was done with one major addition; the inclusion of a tower and cupola and even this was supposed to earn its keep as an astronomical observatory. Construction began in 1750 and when Cassels died a year later his work was carried on by John Ensor.

Mosse took on the role of Hospital Master, a post he held for only two years before he died from some unnamed disease. The hospital he founded did survive thanks to Mosse's sound financial provisions. In 1764 Ensor built the Round or Rotunda Rooms which gave the hospital its popular name.

The chief architectural glory of the Rotunda Hospital is one the general public, although not excluded, rarely see. It is the chapel which has the finest example of baroque plaster work in Ireland and easily on a par with the best in Bavaria or Austria. The stucco was designed by Barthelemy Cramillion and the work executed by the Francini Brothers.

II

Thanks in no small measure to Dr. Bartholomew Mosse the medical establishment embraced midwifery as a respectable profession and the Rotunda Hospital went from strength to strength. More space was needed. The west colonnade was filled in and topped by a three storey extension tastefully matching the original granite stonework. The east colonnade connecting the former Ambassador Cinema has remained untouched.

Later wings, especially the large ornate Thomas Plunkett Cairns building of 1895, were added by which time there was little left of the former pleasure gardens. Even less remained after the Garden of Remembrance, dedicated to those who died for Irish Freedom, was opened on the north side of Parnell (formerly Rutland) Square in 1966.

Infant mortality was high in the early days of the hospital and while facilities were acceptable then they were abysmal by todays standards. Disease and fever took their toll and sanitation was almost non-existent. As medical knowledge grew and better procedures were adopted the short comings of the hospital were tackled. Water closets were at last installed in 1855 and twenty years later, and not before its time, nurses were obliged to wash their hands with carbolic soap.

Since the foundation of the Rotunda, (generally believed to be the first maternity hospital in these islands) 650,000 babies have been born within its portals and it is now world famous as a graduate and post graduate teaching centre.

Patrick Conway's pub across the road from the Rotunda has existed since 1745, the year Mosse founded his first lying-in hospital. It probably provided a welcome refuge for the staff of the early Rotunda and indeed it still performs the same service although dressed now in its 19th century Victorian shopfront.

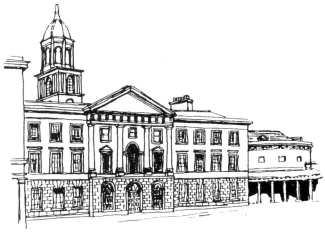

ROTUNDA HOSPITAL

LYING-IN HOSPITAL, DUBLIN 1796

ROTUNDA HOSPITAL, DUBLIN 1990

16

Ambassador & Gate (Rotunda New Rooms)

I

One of the first effects of building the new Lying-in Hospital and supporting pleasure gardens was that they attracted more development. Rutland Square (named after a Viceroy who delighted in frequenting the entertainments) was soon surrounded by elegant houses occupied by a great number of peers, members of Parliament and bishops.

To offer even better accommodation The Round Room or Rotunda was built in 1764. Further extensions in the 1780s embraced the New Assembly Rooms (site of the present Gate Theatre) a remodelled Rotunda and two new pavillions (one is seen on the left of Malton's plate). Richard Johnston, brother of the more famous Francis the designer of the G.P.O., and James Gandon were the architects associated with these new works.

The Rotunda Assembly Rooms could now offer the eighty feet diameter Round Room which could hold 2,000 people, a ballroom, card room, supper and tea and coffee rooms, a hall for sedan chairs and other ancilliary rooms. The gardens had gravelled walks, open areas for band recitals and the like, an artificial waterfall, illuminations for night time use and a bowling green. In 1783 the great Volunteer Convention was held in the Rotunda. The convention was an expression of the new sense of confidence and independence from Britain being then experienced by the Protestant ascendancy.

II

Once the depressing effects of the 1800 Act of Union took hold, the Gardens and Assembly Rooms began to feel the economic downturn. The higher social classes commenced to abandon the north side of the city and Rutland Square and more especially its environs rapidly declined. The Gardens continued to be used for great social occasions until the 1850s but with less frequency and success and ultimately the encroachment from necessary building extensions to the hospital forced their closure.

The Round and Assembly Rooms continued as designed for the whole century especially in providing theatre and variety shows. Shortly after the turn of the century the Round Room was converted into the Ambassador Cinema which remained in business until two years ago and now lies fallow. In 1929 Hilton Edwards and Michael MacLiammoir took over the Great Supper Room as the Gate Theatre. The downstairs ballroom continued to function into the 1960s and has recently been restored as the Pillar Room but awaits further remedial work before being reopened.

Just below the Gate Theatre is an attractive polished stone drinking fountain, one of the many which used to adorn the city's streets and have now been reduced to a few examples.

DRINKING FOUNTAIN

ROTUNDA NEW ROOMS 1796

AMBASSADOR AND GATE THEATRE, DUBLIN 1990

17

St. Catherine's Church

I

Originally St. Catherine's was a 12th century chapel of Ease to the Abbey of St. Thomas with the present church on Thomas Street replacing the medieval structure in 1765. Design was by John Smyth, architect of St. Thomas' in Marlborough St. (destroyed in the Civil War of 1922) and the Poolbeg Lighthouse.

The granite facade executed in the Doric style is considered by many to be the finest example of church architecture in Dublin. Smyth must have been very crestfallen when the raising of his graceful spire was abandoned due to lack of finance. Only the capped stump remains to this day but in a curious way it stamps the church with a pleasing individuality.

Thomas Street was a principal highway to the west and the area around St. Catherine's became fairly densely populated, mostly with less privileged communities than were to be found in other city centre parishes. The Rev. James Whitelaw, vicar of St. Catherine's around the time of Malton, carried out a census of the city and found that the general district around his church contained vast numbers of indigent and unemployed people living in wretchedly cramped and squalid conditions. He spent much of his life working to bring relief to the suffering poor and his body now lies buried in the vaults of St. Catherine's.

Malton's print certainly reveals a less prosperous street scene than is found in the majority of his other views. The houses look robust and modern enough but they lack an air of elegance as also do the passers by. The ubiquitous water barrel cart is in this case supplemented by a cart carrying barrels of what one might reasonably suppose to be porter from the nearby Guinness Brewery.

The 19th century started inauspiciously for St. Catherine's when a scaffold was erected in 1803 outside the church to hang Robert Emmet following his dismal attempted Revolution. As the century drew on the parish went into further social decline but, although growing ever fewer in number, the Protestant community clung tenaciously on until recent times.

However, by 1967 the Church of Ireland could no longer sustain the parish and the building was handed over to Dublin Corporation who leased it to the Bell Tower Trust, a voluntary group. A long litany of structural woes from years of under-maintenance, including dry and wet rot, perishing stonework and collapsing ceilings then began to reveal themselves. The Trust repaired the organ in 1975 at a cost of £25,000 and further monies were spent by Dublin Corporation and the South Inner City Community Development Association.

Additional financial support from public and commercial sources was sought unsuccessfully and further refurbishment was abandoned in the late 80s. Vandals have since smashed the organ and stripped the guttering with the result that there is now severe water saturation of the stonework which will cause damage beyond repair if not soon rectified. Estimated cost of rehabilitation is £250,000.

Dublin Corporation recently placed St. Catherine's on the market in the hope that a sympathetic new owner will bring the church, albeit in a different guise, back literally from the grave.

Replacing the 18th century sedan shelters are the modern-day bus shelters. The bus is, along with the motor car, the successor to the carriages which appear in almost all of Malton's pictures. Bus Atha Cliath — Dublin Bus operates a fleet of 800 double and single deck buses throughout the city.

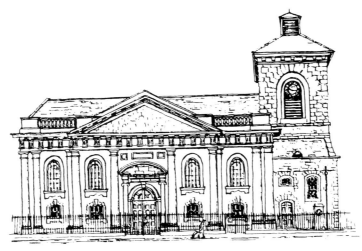

ST. CATHERINE'S, THOMAS STREET

SAINT CATHERINE'S CHURCH, DUBLIN 1797

SAINT CATHERINE'S CHURCH, DUBLIN 1990

18

View up the Liffey (Marine School)

I

The Vikings built the first rudimentary quayside on the Liffey made from banks of earth fronted by wooden revetments. Successive embankments, each one further towards the centre of the river in an attempt to increase the water depth, were constructed by the Norsemen and their Norman successors but these arrangements were finally displaced in the early 14th century by a masonry harbour wall built roughly in line with present-day Wood Quay.

Dublin Port continued to be troubled by silting and tidal shallows and the first concerted attempt to address the many problems of access resulted in the foundation of the Ballast Office in 1707. In the largest engineering project the city had seen to date the quay walls were extended to Ringsend, the North and South Walls were built and lighthouses erected to guide shipping through the treacherous sandbars. By 1794 the Custom House and Carlisle (O'Connell) Bridge had been opened and all shipping was now located on that part of the river shown in Malton's print. In 1786 the Ballast Office was replaced by the Corporation for Preserving and Improving the Port of Dublin otherwise known simply as the Ballast Board.

The Marine School (on the left of Malton's picture), quaintly named the Hibernian Nursery for the Support and Education of the Orphans and Children of Mariners, was opened in 1773 on land leased on Sir John Rogerson's Quay. The institution prepared boys for service with the Merchant Marine or the Royal Navy.

Shipbuilding had been a tradition in Dublin since Viking days and Malton has included the stern of a vessel being constructed in the yard of Matthew Cardiff.

Following a fire the Marine School moved out in 1872 and the building fulfilled a variety of uses mostly as a warehouse until the main central section was demolished in 1979.

The Ballast Board was reconstituted in 1868 as the Dublin Port and Docks Board. Development of the port continued apace. Deep berth facilities were opened at Alexandra Basin where the main activity is based today. Dublin Port has declined somewhat in recent years but there are plans to attract new business. Currently it receives 4,000 ships annually handling 7.3 million tonnes of freight and 650,000 passengers. There are 9km. of berthage.

On the central riverfront itself most of the cranes have been removed, new uses are being found for the warehouses and depots, waterfront housing is becoming popular and leisure boating is likely to increase. Even the gasometer, a city landmark for generations, is now redundant and is earmarked for removal. The new Financial Services Centre will soon dominate the skyline beside the Custom House. Liberty Hall, just visible behind the Custom House is the city's only skyscraper and its ugly plainness and inherent shabbyness continues to be, in the writer's view, a blot on the cityscape.

ANNA LIVIA, DETAIL FROM CUSTOM HOUSE

THE MARINE SCHOOL, DUBLIN 1796

VIEW UP THE LIFFEY, DUBLN 1990

19

Leinster House

I

James Fitzgerald, when he became the 20th Earl of Kildare in 1744, engaged Richard Cassels, the architect of his country seat, Carton House near Maynooth, to build a show-piece mansion in the Molesworth Fields in Dublin. Work started in 1745 on what was to become the largest of the great town houses. Its presence on what was previously green fields inspired a great relocation of fashionable living to the south east of the city, an influence which is felt to this day.

Kildare House, renamed Leinster House after the earl was made Duke of Leinster in 1766, was curious in that it presented a country house entrance across its wide expanse of lawn to the Merrion Square side and a city town house entrance on its western facade facing Molesworth Street. Perhaps the good earl couldn't make up his mind whether he preferred living in the country or in the city.

The house remained in the Fitzgerald family for about seventy years with Lord Edward Fitzgerald, a leading rebel of the 1798 Rebellion and an embarrassment to his family, being perhaps its most celebrated resident.

Like many of the great families who sold their city mansions after the Act of Union in 1800, the Fitzgeralds sold Leinster House to the Dublin Society (later the Royal Dublin Society) in 1814. Foremost in the fields of arts and sciences the Dublin Society amassed a great library, started a world famous School of Art and from 1830 ran agricultural shows on the grounds of Leinster Lawn.

For the Great (Industrial) Exhibition of 1853 a huge glass and steel structure was erected on Leinster Lawn to which Queen Victoria and Prince Albert paid a visit. A fine statue to Albert now stands on the site. A significant art collection put together for the exhibition went on to become the nucleus for the National Art Gallery built on the grounds in 1864. The Natural History Museum had already been built on the opposite side of Leinster Lawn in 1857.

On the Kildare Street side of Leinster House to its right and left were built from 1877 the National Museum and the National Library. By an Act of the same year the responsibility for the museums, the art school and the Society's botanic gardens passed to the Government and in 1922 Leinster House itself was purchased from the R.D.S. to accommodate the Dáil and Seanad.

Since then a multitude of improvements, reconstructions and additions were made including, most recently, an in-depth restoration of the Seanad chamber. Redesigned as a picture gallery by James Wyatt in 1755 this room suffered structural damage as a result. Commencing in 1986 remedial action was carried out and the beautifully plastered ceiling was saved and refurbished. The total cost for these works was £1.1 million.

LEINSTER HOUSE GATES

LEINSTER HOUSE, DUBLIN 1792

LEINSTER HOUSE, DUBLIN 1990

20

Municipal Gallery (Charlemont House)

James Caulfield, first Earl of Charlemont, decided in 1762 to build a showpiece townhouse on the northern side of Parnell Square then known as Palace Row. He bought three building lots to give himself the required space and engaged a famous English architect of the day, Sir William Chambers.

The finished house, faced in Portland stone and rustic granite and flanked on either side by balustraded curving screen walls, was one of the most splendid mansions in the city. It vied with Leinster House as the centre for social gatherings with Lord Charlemont himself being a very congenial host. Visitors to his residence were entertained royally and could also enjoy his vast library and his superb collection of art and artefacts purchased on his Grand European Tour.

By any standard Lord Charlemont was a remarkable man. Apart from his extensive art collection and his generous patronage to artists he commissioned the Casino in Marino, now acknowledged to be among the finest buildings of its genre in the world. He was a founding member of the Royal Irish Academy and was commander-in-chief of the Irish Volunteers, formed as a Protestant force to repel any Napoleonic invasion. A mounted unit of this force can be seen outside Charlemont House in Malton's painting.

On the left side of Malton's view is one of a pair of shelters for sedan-chair men, a kind of eighteenth century taxi-rank.

II

Lord Charlemont died in 1799 and the house passed to his heirs who ultimately sold it to the Government in 1870 who used it as the General Registry Office for births, marriages and deaths. In 1929 Dublin Corporation received the building specifically to house a modern art collection. To this end the front part of the house was retained but the rear was demolished to make way for new gallery floors.

Various improvements and remedial work have since been undertaken on a regular basis. Extra gallery, and restaurant space, a restorers' room and service areas have been added. A current refurbishment includes a general redecoration, replacement of window glass with special ultra-violet filters and the installation of sophisticated lighting.

Officially named the Hugh Lane Gallery it commemorates the man who bequeathed his fabled collection of Continental masters to Dublin in 1905. Difficulties arose for a suitable permanent gallery and Sir Hugh Lane grew impatient and selected instead the National Gallery in London. He died aboard the Lusitania in 1915 but in an unwitnessed codicil to his will he reversed his previous decision in favour of Dublin again. A dispute obviously arose and an agreement was finally reached whereby the paintings would be shared by both Dublin and London.

Today the gallery possesses, in large measure thanks to Lane, a good representation of 19th century art including works by Constable, Monet, Degas, Courbet, Corot, Fantin-Latour, Mancini and Irish painters Jack Yeats and Nathaniel Hone.

The old sedan-chair shelters disappeared in 1943 and this area of the former Rotunda pleasure gardens is now occupied by the Garden of Remembrance. The large houses on the right of the modern view are presently being totally restored to become an Irish Writers' Museum and a Living Writers' Centre.

No. 18 on the far right was last occupied as a residence by the Jameson family of whiskey fame.

MUNICIPAL GALLERY

CHARLEMONT HOUSE, DUBLIN 1793

MUNICIPAL GALLERY, DUBLIN 1990

21

Powerscourt Townhouse Centre (Powerscourt House)

I

Eighteenth century Dublin was graced by several significant mansions such as Tyrone House, Clonmel House, Belvedere House, Aldborough House, Leinster House, Charlemont House, and of course the imposing Powerscourt House.

The third Viscount Powerscourt, who already lived in sumptuous splendour in his vast Wicklow estate decided in 1771 to employ Robert Mack to design a townhouse which would be a show piece. The site he selected was less than useful in achieving an appreciation of the intended grandeur as the enclosed narrowness of the street prevents a decent view except at an acute angle. Even the width of the street in Malton's view is probably exaggerated somewhat.

Powerscourt House, completed in 1774, boasted a great staircase by James McCullagh and fine plasterwork by Michael Stapleton. The left hand side entrance led to the kitchens while the one on the right opened to the stables.

The house on the right was built for the Society of Artists in 1765-71 and contained an exhibition room. In 1791 the City Council moved in when the Tholsel was found to be unsafe.

II

The Powerscourt family sold the mansion in 1807 to the Commissioners of Stamp Duties for £15,000 and it became the Stamp Office. A range of additional office buildings were then erected to the rear of the big house to form a quadrangle.

In 1835 Ferrier Pollock, wholesale drapers, purchased Powerscourt House. This firm maintained the building in good condition until it was sold again in the late 1970s.

This time the buyer was a development company, Power Securities (now Power Corporation), who assured the future of Powerscourt House by initiating a sensitive redevelopment. The quadrangle was roofed in and restaurants, craft shops and the like turned the complex into a vibrant commercial and social centre. The scheme has since won several awards.

The line of the building to the left of Powerscourt House is still the same as in Malton's day with many of the buildings still original. Council meetings were held in the City Assembly Rooms (the former premises of the Society of Artists) until 1852 and today the building houses the collection of the Civic Museum.

Coppinger Row, between the Civic Museum and Powerscourt House, is now part of an extensive pedestrian system centred on Grafton Street.

POWERSCOURT TOWNHOUSE CENTRE

POWERSCOURT HOUSE, DUBLIN 1795

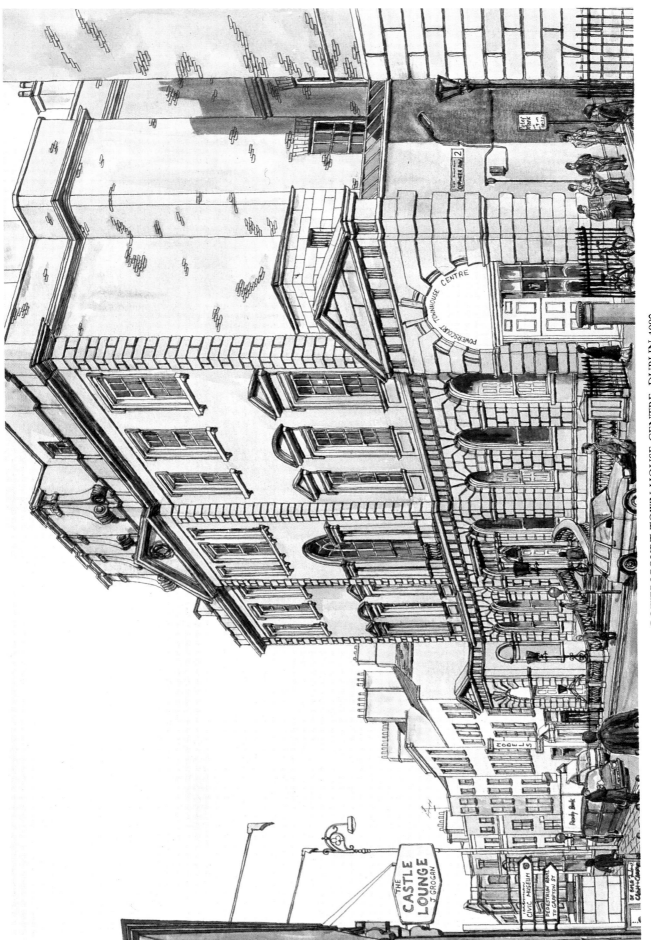

POWERSCOURT TOWN HOUSE CENTRE, DUBLIN 1990

22

View from Capel Street

I

This print is full of street life, social commentary and local colour.

An army contingent from the Royal (Collins) Barracks is riding with bugles sounding on its way to Dublin Castle. A lamplighter is cleaning a globe and filling a container with a fresh supply of fish blubber. Beggars and the lowly mix uneasily with the wealthier strands of society. Shoeless poor children rub shoulders with the well dressed young of the rich. Dogs are obviously popular.

The road surface is in good order and footpaths are well laid stone flags. Two lotteries, one the Old State Lottery with the Irish Harp as its symbol and the other the Military State Lottery, have their offices in the left hand side buildings. A ship, tilted on the low tide, lies at anchor in front of Thomas Burgh's Old Custom House which was built in 1707. George Semple's elegant hump-backed bridge, complete with built-in sentry posts, was opened in 1755 and leads into Parliament Street. This street was the result of the Wide Streets Commission's first endeavour in 1758. It was an important roadway as it led directly to Dublin Castle. The Royal Exchange closes the vista at the top end.

II

In some respects very little change over the last two hundred years has occurred to the general arrangements of the vista but of course individual buildings have disappeared. The main absentees are the frontages along the south quays which have arguably been replaced by finer Victorian buildings.

Both Parliament Street and Capel Street, once very fashionable commercial and residential thoroughfares, have suffered a decline but may be set again for at least some limited resurgence. Sadly, almost nobody lives anymore on these streets and any worthwhile renewal has to include residential elements.

The buildings on the left of Capel Street are still the original, as is the Royal Exchange, now City Hall. Semple's hump-backed bridge was demolished in 1874 to make way for the flatter surfaced ironwork Grattan Bridge adorned with its decorative seahorse lanterns.

SUNLIGHT CHAMBERS & CAPEL ST. BRIDGE

VIEW FROM CAPEL STREET, DUBLIN 1797

VIEW FROM CAPEL STREET, DUBLIN 1990

23

St. Stephen's Green

I

Parks in Malton's time were more parade grounds for the promenading rich than places used for recreation by all and sundry. St. Stephen's Green was no exception and was in fact, for a time, a principal resort for the public display of the latest high fashions.

From medieval times St. Stephen's Green, named after the chapel of a nearby leper hospital, was used as grazing land for livestock. In 1663 Dublin Corporation set out the central 27 acres and enclosed the area with a stone wall. The remaining 33 acres were sold as building lots, the rents were to support the walling of the green and the building of the Blue Coat Hospital.

Throughout the 18th century the interior of the Green continued to be used for pasturage and the level parkland also proved ideal for military parades, public assemblies, demonstrations and occasional executions.

In the background of Malton's lively scene (the figures are particularly well executed in this example) can be seen John Nost's equestrian statue of George II, (blown up in the early part of this century) and the gracious houses on the east and south sides of the Green. The landscaped paths running along the four sides were known as Monk's Walk (East), Leeson's Walk (South), French Walk (West) and Beaux' Walk (North).

II

From the beginning of the 19th century the public was excluded from the Green unless a key was rented. This high-handed approach was highly resented but nothing was done about it and the park itself fell into bad times and suffered from neglect. In 1877 Sir Arthur Guinness, later Lord Ardilaun, personally paid off the Green's accumulated debts and secured the passage of an Act of Parliament to turn it into a public park in the care of the Office of Public Works.

Within the next three years the park as we know it today was laid out including the artificial waterfall, the stone bridge, the formal flower beds and fountains, the walks and the superintendent's lodge. In July 1880 St. Stephen's Green was opened to the public.

Improvements have continued down the years interrupted only once by a major historic event; the occupation of the Green in 1916 by units of the Irish Citizen Army and Irish Volunteers under Michael Mallin and Countess Markiewicz.

There are fourteen commemorative statues and memorials located at strategic points around the Green including the Fusiliers' Arch (which would be behind the viewer of the present picture), statues to Lord Ardilaun, Robert Emmet, Wolfe Tone, and James Joyce and a bust of Countess Markiewicz.

Recently more innovations and improvements have been carried out costing over £260,000. A new garden for the blind is planned, two new exotic timber shelters have been built and a modern children's playground with a unique safety surface has been opened.

FUSILIERS' ARCH

SAINT STEPHEN'S GREEN, DUBLIN 1796

SAINT STEPHEN'S GREEN, DUBLIN 1990

24

Collins Barracks (The Barracks)

I

For over 500 years, as was common in other countries, troops based in Dublin were billeted in a variety of inconvenient places including castles, keeps, camps, churches, requisitioned public buildings and private dwellings. This led to all sorts of problems including the enforcement of discipline and rapid assembly of units. To overcome these disadvantages Colonel Thomas Burgh (architect of Trinity Library and Dr. Stephen's Hospital) was asked to design a specific group of buildings within their own compound and thus in 1706 the new (later Royal) Barracks was opened.

Initially there was only the central or Royal Square but later in the century the Cavalry Square, the Little Square and the Palatine Square were added.

The growing instability of English political sway in Ireland often required the presence of large numbers of soldiers and the Royal Barracks proved admirable for accommodating them. A commentator in 1735 described the complex as the "most magnificent, largest and most commodious of its kind in Europe". By the time Malton executed his drawing it could hold 5,000 men. The Barracks supplied guard troops for postings all over the city.

II

Troops from the Royal Barracks were extensively used to crush the Rebellion of 1798 and many of the executed rebels were buried in a field between the barracks and the River Liffey which became known as the Croppies' Hole. The field is still there and the fountain in the Croppies' Memorial Park nearby commemorates the dead.

The last British soldiers to leave Dublin in 1922 were those who vacated the Royal Barracks on the 17th December. It was then renamed Collins Barracks in memory of Michael Collins, assassinated commander-in-chief of the Irish Free State army.

It is believed that Collins Barracks is the world's oldest purpose-built barracks in continuous occupation and the Government's stated plan to now close it must be deeply regretted. There are other installations on prime sites more worthy of closure which if sold on the open market would easily fund a total modernisation of Collins. It would be an unenlightened decision and a tragic loss to sever the military connection with such an historically significant barracks. In an effort to persuade the Department of Defence to change its mind Dublin City Council decided in October this year to list the main buildings on Preservation List 1 and the entrance gates, railings and boundary walls on List 2. Regretably these preservation orders can be overruled by Government when dealing with state property.

The farms in front of Malton's Barracks have long since been buried under the buildings of the Guinness Brewery whose presence made it too difficult to represent the modern view from the same panoramic perspective. Instead it is taken from just inside the gates of the brewery overlooking Victoria Quay.

COLLINS BARRACKS

THE BARRACKS, DUBLIN 1795

COLLINS BARRACKS, DUBLIN 1990

25

View of Dublin from the Magazine Fort

I

Originally part of the Abbey of Kilmainham the Phoenix Park was first enclosed with walls by the Duke of Ormonde in 1662. A herd of fallow deer was introduced for the pleasure of Royal hunting parties. From 1745 the Earl of Chesterfield introduced more improvements including opening the park to the public. Mansions were built for the Viceroy, the Secretary and Under-Secretary. Gates and lodges secured the perimeter entrances.

The Magazine Fort was built on St. Thomas' Hill the site of Phoenix House, the 17th century residence of the Viceroys. Built to house munitions the fort was erected between 1732 and 1735 by the Duke of Wharton.

St. Thomas' Hill was a popular vantage point to view the panorama of Dublin city. Clearly visible in Malton's painting is the River Liffey then bordered by green fields until it enters the city centre proper. Also prominent is the village of Islandbridge and just beyond the Royal Hospital in Kilmainham. To the left of the Royal Hospital can be seen the tower of Dr. Steven's Hospital, the spires of churches including St. Patrick's and the dome of the Four Courts. On the extreme left is the Royal Military Infirmary.

The people depicted in the painting are obviously out to relax and enjoy the open spaces.

II

Throughout the next century the city developed across the green fields of Malton's view. Within the park itself many trees were planted. The author's painting could not be drawn from quite the same spot as Malton selected because now a woodland totally obscures the cityscape. The current perspective is taken from the southern side of the hill instead of from the eastern side in front of the entrance to the Magazine Fort.

In a little exercise of artistic licence the contemporary landscape has been somewhat foreshortened to help identify the features. In addition to the landmarks already in place in Malton's time there is now the Wellington Monument, Heuston Railway Terminus, the Guinness Brewery, the spires and towers of more recent churches and the increased numbers of buildings in general.

The Phoenix Park itself is still the great outdoor parkland it always was. A new management plan was launched in 1986 by the Office of Public Works and is now well underway. It aims to make dramatic improvements to the scenic beauty of the park and to enhance the facilities for its enjoyment. Within a span of ten years 20,000 new trees will be planted, monuments and a ruined castle will be restored and better traffic management will be introduced. The gas lighting system has been upgraded and extended, the original gate piers at the Parkgate Street entrance have been re-erected. A series of heritage trails have been established and even the horse-drawn carriages were re-introduced.

The Magazine Fort is also being gradually improved with a long term view that it would be opened to the public.

MAGAZINE FORT, PHOENIX PARK

VIEW OF DUBLIN FROM THE MAGAZINE FORT, 1795

VIEW OF DUBLIN FROM THE MAGAZINE FORT, 1990

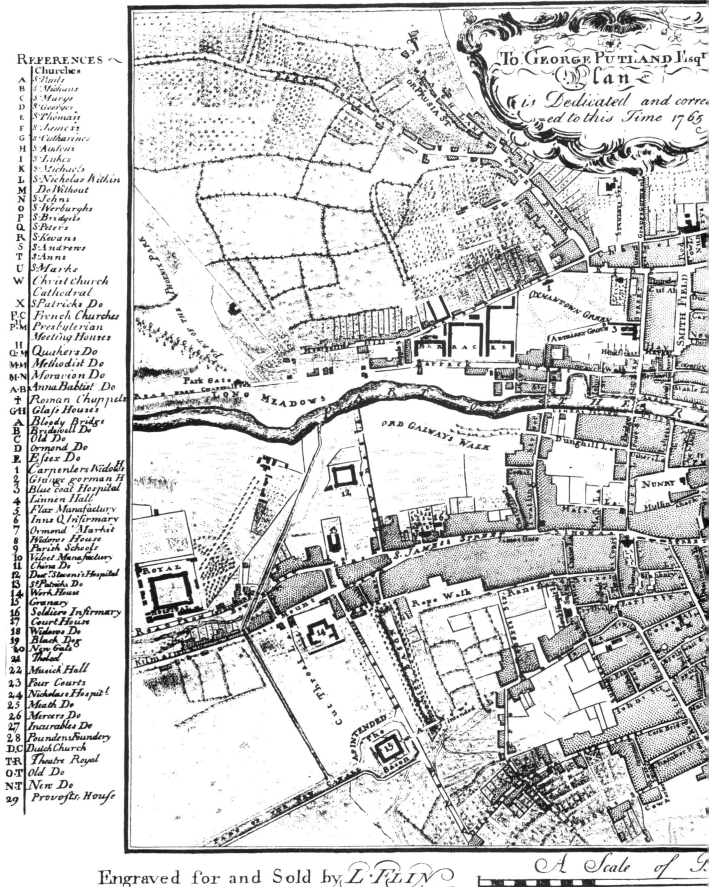

A Plan of the City and Suburbs

Engraved for and Sold by L. FLIN

(Reproduced courtesy of the Civic Museum, Dublin)

106

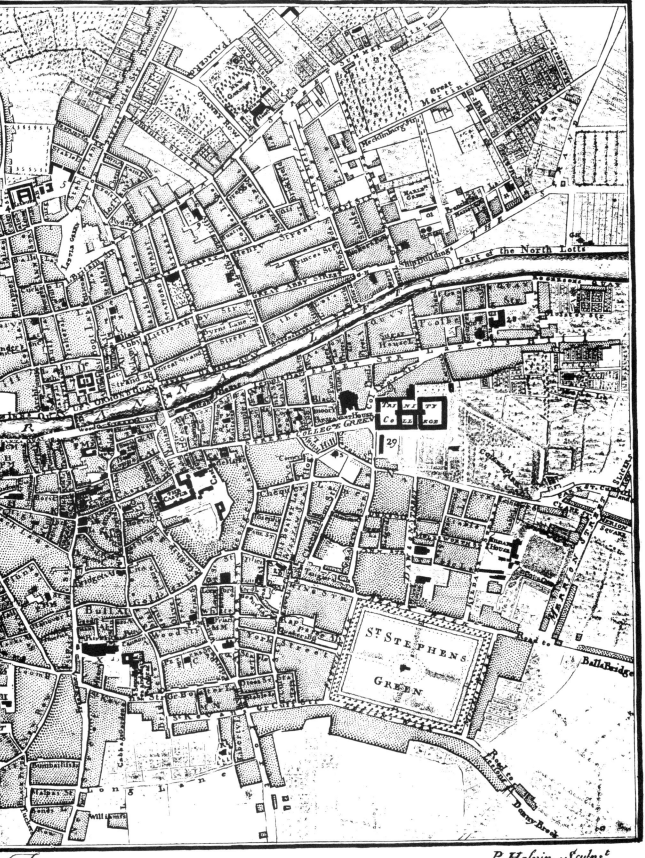

Dublin By J. Rocque Reduc'd from his large PLAN

Feet
4000

at the Bible in Castle Street & I. WILLIAMS

P. Halpin Sculpt.
Skinner.

Other titles by the Author:

DUBLIN TODAY   The Irish Times, Dublin 1984
Casebound ISBN 0 907011 13 6

DUBLIN BE PROUD   Chadworth Limited, Dublin 1987
Paperback ISBN 0 95 125 10 07
Casebound ISBN 0 95 125 10 15
Special Bound Limited Edition 0 95 125 10 23

Biography

Born in Dublin in 1944 Pat Liddy held his first one-man art exhibition in 1982.

His series in the Irish Times, which ran from 1982 to 1989, highlighted the architectural and historic features of the city in words and drawings. This became the title of his first bestselling book "Dublin Today" and the basis of his second major show "Celebrating Dublin" in 1985.

Pat's second book "Dublin Be Proud" published in October 1987 to launch the Dublin Millennium became an outstanding bestseller and resulted in successful shows in Dublin and abroad in Brussels, Zurich and the United States.

Other works included an exhibition of watercolour paintings, drawings and photographs held in the Chester Beatty Library, executed during a tour of China with the traditional Irish musicians "The Chieftains".

He has also contributed to many journals and books including Heritage Trails and tourist guides.